Learning About Caring

Meet Karina!

Karina the Kangaroo stands for caring. Her name is from the Spanish word for "caring." Karina cares deeply about others and has a great capacity to empathize with their feelings. She is always ready to listen, lend a hand, or speak an encouraging word. Karina carries an endless supply of goodies which she gives to those in need.

Ideas for Teaching Caring at Home

Here are a few simple ideas for helping your child develop a strong character based on good values:

1. Use the words *caring*, *kind*, and *considerate* as you do each activity page with your child. This way your child will become familiar with concepts related to caring. Talk about how people show their concern for the well-being of others, using examples from your own life and the news. Newspapers often have a regular feature about people who are making a difference in their community. Regularly read this feature to your child.

2. Tell your child that you want him or her to be caring. Praise caring behavior and discourage selfish behavior. If you notice your child, yourself, or others acting selfishly, point this out and talk about it.

3. Make a "We Care" scrapbook with your child. When your child or other family members are involved in helping others, record the events and take pictures. Honor and praise your child as you would if your child received top grades or excelled in a sport. This shows your child that you value caring. Encourage your child to generate his or her own ideas for helping others and assist your child in carrying them out.

4. Be careful and conscious about setting a good example of caring through your own actions—both large and small. What you do and don't do sends a message to your child.

What Will Karina Teach?

Here are some concepts about caring that Karina will help your child understand.

People who are caring . . .
- are concerned about the well-being of others
- are not mean, selfish, or too busy to help
- have empathy—the ability to share in another person's feelings
- voluntarily give money or time to help those in need
- are forgiving of others

Using the T.E.A.M. Strategy

The T.E.A.M. strategy, developed by the CHARACTER COUNTS℠ Coalition is an effective approach for developing character.

TEACH: Teach your child that his or her character counts—that personal success and happiness will depend on who your child is on the inside, not on what he or she has or how he or she looks.

ENFORCE: Reward your child's good behavior and discourage all instances of bad behavior by imposing fair, consistent consequences that prove you are serious about character.

ADVOCATE: Be an advocate for character. Don't be neutral about the importance of character nor casual about improper conduct.

MODEL: Be careful and self-conscious about setting a good example in everything you say and do. Everything you do, and don't do sends a message about your values.

Remember, the development of good character is a process. You are building character a day at a time and often the path is two steps forward and one step back. The ongoing efforts you make will be rewarded as your child becomes a person of good character!

Karina Cares

Connect the dots from **A** to **Z**.

Cut out the pages. Staple them to make a mini-book.

1

Karina the Kangaroo is caring.

2

Karina is kind, helpful, and generous to everyone.

3

Karina always thinks about other people's feelings and needs.

4

Karina does good deeds without thinking about what she will get in return.

Parent: Tell your child that Karina wears a medal of character. Explain that a medal is often given to someone who has done something very good. Say to your child: *Karina has good character. She is kind with her words and actions. She thinks about other people's feelings and needs. She helps others without thinking about what she might get in return. She has earned her medal of character for caring.*

I Am Kind

Look at each picture.
Does the picture show a child who is being kind?
Circle **yes** if it does. Circle **no** if it does not.

yes   no

yes   no

yes   no

yes   no

yes   no

yes   no

Parent: Explain to your child that children who are kind care about the feelings of others. Talk with your child about what is happening in each picture. Ask your child how it makes him or her feel when someone is unkind.

BV30005 Caring

Pets Need Love and Care

Listen to the story.

> Patrick got a new puppy.
> He feeds the puppy food.
> He gives the puppy water.
> He brushes the puppy's fur.
> He gives the puppy lots of love.

Draw lines to complete each sentence.

water

Patrick got a new _____.

puppy

He feeds the puppy _____.

food

He gives the puppy _____.

love

He brushes the puppy's _____.

He gives the puppy lots of _____.

fur

Parent: Talk with your child about how Patrick takes care of his puppy. Explain that pets have needs like people do. They need care and love. Ask your child *What would happen if Patrick didn't take care of his puppy?*

BV30005 Caring

Don't Be Cruel

Listen to the story and each question.
Answer the question aloud.
Trace the question mark at the end of the question.

What did Emma get?

What did Logan say?

How do you think Emma feels?

Was Logan being a caring friend?

Parent Ask if anything like this has ever happened to your child and let him or her tell you about it. Have your child pretend to be each child and think about how he or she would feel in the situation. Then help your child understand that a caring person does not say things that are mean, cruel, or insensitive. Ask your child *What could Logan have said instead?*

I Am Thankful

Listen to each story. Which words show a child who is thankful? Color those words.

Jonathan gave his old bike to his younger cousin Ned.

"I don't want an old bike."

"Thank you! That bike is just the right size for me."

Katie lost a bracelet. Melanie found it and gave it back.

"Thank you for giving back my bracelet."

"Hey, that's mine. Give it back to me."

Gina helped Joey finish raking leaves so he could play baseball.

"Thanks so much. Let me know when I can help you."

"Hurry up. You're too slow."

Parent: Tell your child that caring people are thankful and express gratitude for what people do for them. After reading each story, talk together about the two things the child might say. Then help your child determine which words show a child who is thankful.

Karina Does Good Deeds

Listen to each story. Draw a line to match each story to the good deed Karina did.

Some kids do not have clean clothes for school.

Karina helps wash kids' clothes at the school laundry.

The bakery burned down in a fire. The owners need money to rebuild.

Karina helps Jason learn to read.

Jason wants to learn how to read.

Karina gives money to the bakery owners.

Parent: Tell your child that caring people often give money, time, support, and comfort just for the sake of making someone else's life better, not because they are getting something in return. Ask your child *How do you think Karina feels when she does good deeds?*

Karina Cares About You

Listen to each sentence.
Draw a line to the matching picture.

Austus is sick. Karina writes a get-well card for him.

Kupa has a broken leg. Karina visits her.

Shinrai is afraid to go to the dentist. Karina goes with her.

Guisto is sad because his cat is missing. Karina helps him look for the cat.

BV30005 Caring

Jenna Helps People In Need

Cut out the pictures. Paste them in order.

There was a fire on Jenna's street.
A family lost their home and all their things.
Jenna had five dollars in her piggy bank.
She bought crayons and color books.
She gave them to the kids in the family.

1

2

3

Parent: Remind your child that caring people share with those who are victims of some kind of tragedy or disaster. Next time your child is made aware of such a situation, talk together about what you can do to help the people in need.

10 BV30005 Caring

How Do They Feel?

Caring people think about the feelings of others.
Cut, match, and paste.

Parent: This page focuses on the concept of empathy. Help your child develop empathy by discussing how the children in each situation on this page feel. Then encourage your child to share how he or she would feel in each situation.

I Can Forgive

Caring people try to forgive people when they do something wrong. Listen to each story.

You made us lose.

Lynn is angry because Ben dropped the ball.

I'm sorry. I shouldn't blame you.

Lynn tells Ben she's sorry.

Which words show Ben forgiving? **Color them.**

I forgive you. Let's get our treats.

I don't ever want to see you again.

Matthew teases Jed and hurts his feelings.

Matthew tells Jed he's sorry.

Which words show Jed forgiving? **Color them.**

You're not my friend anymore.

I forgive you.

Parent: This page introduces the concept of forgiveness. Explain to your child that although it may be hard, caring people often forgive others for their shortcomings. Give examples of times when you've forgiven others.

Using Caring Words

Look at each picture. Listen to the words.
Are the words caring?
Write **yes** if they are. Write **no** if they are not.

Parent: Encourage your child to tell what he or she sees happening in each picture. Invite your child to act out different scenarios to help model how to use caring words.

BV30005 Caring

Who Is It?

She is helpful and kind. Who is it?

helpful—**blue**   kind—brown

Parent: Tell your child that you expect him or her to be helpful and kind just like Karina the Kangaroo. Talk about how to be helpful and kind to both people you know and people you do not know.

Lend a Helping Hand

Listen to the story.

Kristin made cupcakes for the people
at the nursing home.
It was too much work to do alone.
Jack wanted to go outside to play.
He stayed inside and helped Kristin.

caring

Name the letters in the word **caring**
Find the letters in the picture. Circle them.

Parent: Explain to your child that caring people are never too busy to lend a helping hand. Point out that caring people often give up their chance to do something fun in order to help out someone who needs it.

Find the Words

Caring people feel what other people feel. If someone feels sad or happy, a caring person feels sad or happy too.

Find and circle the words.
The words go across and down.

Word Box

caring

happy

sad

mad

merry

d	b	x	q	w	p	c	y
f	s	x	l	i	n	a	s
h	a	p	p	y	d	r	e
o	d	l	a	t	i	i	g
i	m	a	d	c	z	n	b
m	e	r	r	y	g	g	l

Parent: Discuss the meaning of *empathy*. Talk to your child about the saying "Take a walk in their shoes." Let your child know that people who really care feel sad when others are sad and feel happy when others are happy. Have your child think of a time when he or she felt happy or sad because of something that happened to another person.

Giving to Others

Karina has some gifts for a poor family. Find a path to help Karina take the gifts to their home.

Parent: Remind your child that caring people give to those in need. Perhaps your child has participated in Toys for Tots or a similar gift-giving program. If not, you may wish to look for an opportunity to involve your child in such a program.

I Care for Others

Look at the pictures. Read the words.
Circle the ways you care for others.

say kind things

give gifts and cards

help people in need

visit a lonely person

share how someone feels

Parent: Explain to your child that it is important to be concerned about the well-being of other people. Remind your child that there are many things he or she can do to show caring to other people.

BV30005 Caring

Caring for Your Family

Each child is doing something to show caring.
Draw a line to what each child needs.

What does Summer need to wrap a gift for Dad?

What does Sam need to make a card for Grandma?

What does Brook need to read to her sister?

What does Nathan need to play with the dog?

Time to Care

Choose the best title for each picture.
Write the title on the line.

A Cheery Song

A Long Walk

_____

- -

_____

A Gift From Karina

Time to Work

_____

- -

_____

Parent: Remind your child that Karina thinks about what she can do to care for other people. Ask your child if he or she knows someone who is having a hard time. Talk together about something your child can do to show caring to that person.

I Am a Caring Person

Write your name on each line.

_____

- -

_____ is a caring person.

_____

- -

_____ can be kind.

_____

- -

_____ can help others.

_____

- -

_____ can think about others' feelings.

Color the medal of caring.
Draw a picture of yourself wearing it.